BRITISH RAILWAYS
STEAM 1962 - 1966

Malcolm Castledine

BOOK LAW PUBLICATIONS

DEDICATION

To our good friend, the late William (Bill) Arundel, who always showed great interest in my railway photography as he was interested in both steam railways and photography. Thank you Bill - I am now using your Rolleiflex alongside my own.

First published in the United Kingdom
by Book Law Publications 2004
382 Carlton Hill, Nottingham, NG4 1JA
Printed and bound by The Amadeus Press, Cleckheaton, West Yorkshire.

INTRODUCTION

In my previous albums I have tended to regionalise or specify the railway subjects under review. In this album I have moved away from specifics, to a point, and include views captured by my camera during the early 1960's when the steam railway was at its greatest point of transition. Included are views taken on the Eastern, Midland and the Western Regions in England at a time when the old regional boundaries laid down at the start of nationalisation were being moved about to such a bewildering extent that whole groups of engine sheds were 'moved' overnight from one Region to another. Of course, by then most of the steam depots were closing at the rate of a couple each week so whereas in, say, 1961 you could 'shed bash' between fifteen and twenty depots on a really good day, it was impossible to do such a thing by 1963 or 64 without travelling further afield because so many sheds had been closed. However, there was still many establishments open for business and it was around these places where we sought out the surviving steam power, be it operational, stored or simply withdrawn. Although the Southern Region is geographically absent from this album, it is represented by four of its home built

locomotives, albeit three of them in a Rotherham scrapyard. The fourth member of the Southern quartet was actually in steam, and on railtour duty in the days when its appearance, well north of Oxford, still raised many eyebrows not to mention gasps of surprise.

The illustrations herein comprise not only the views taken 'on shed' but also a number 'on works'. There are numerous lineside shots, and scenes from RCTS railtours of yesteryear which were not only a pleasure to take part in but were also exciting because anything could and usually did happen.

In my professional life I was an Engineer with the Central Electricity Generating Board and spent half of my career at Castle Donington Power Station in north-west Leicestershire. Within the confines of the power station boiler house and generating building I dealt with very high pressure steam and its associated machinery but I was also able to indulge my hobby in the station rail yard where steam

locomotives were employed until 1990 shunting coal and oil wagons. In 1985 I was able to take up engine driving at the Rutland Railway Museum where, once again, industrial steam locomotives enabled me to enjoy my passion of steam.

(below) **With nearly 500 tons in tow, steamer No.1 and diesel No.2 get to grips with fourteen loaded HAA wagons on 30th March 1990. Aboard the steamer are Lionel Gadsby and Derek Adkins whilst Jim Bromley has charge of the diesel and shunter John Holmes rides in its less frantic cab. The Castle Donington saddletanks ended up being the last steam locomotives working in British industry and this was their last year of use. By now the steamer carries the Powergen livery.**

(opposite) My place of work for some of my adult life was Castle Donington Power Station where, as the Asst. Mechanical Maintenance Engineer, I was involved with large scale steam engineering. Luckily, the CEGB employed steam locomotion, alongside diesels, to shunt the yard until 1990 and I would often take a stroll amongst the sidings to watch the proceedings as the two little but tough Robert Stephenson & Hawthorn built 0-4-0 saddletanks shunted the coal and oil wagons. This was a perfect place to indulge my combined hobby of photography and watching steam locomotives perform. On Friday 31st May 1985 I took this picture of No.1 being oiled by its driver Ken Reeve during a lull in operations. The bulk of the 1959 commissioned, 600 Megawatt, generating station forms an industrial background in the rural setting of north-west Leicestershire.

O4 class Part 3 No.63764 was the last of the unrebuilt ex-ROD engines working on British Railways. Here at Doncaster shed on 10th October 1965, the 2-8-0 is still in business and would be until the end of February of the following year - a miraculous achievement for any locomotive on the Eastern Region during this period, never mind taking into account that this particular locomotive was built in March 1918 by the North British Locomotive Co. for the Ministry of Munitions. The engine started its main line railway career in May 1928 after it had been purchased from the Government by the LNER for £340 in 1927 along with ninety-nine others of its ilk. Numbered 6581 by the LNER, this engine was allocated to the North Eastern area and spent all of the LNER period working there. Dairycoates was its first depot but in September 1929 it moved to the former Hull & Barnsley shed at Springhead. In the dark days of May 1940 it moved to West Hartlepool and spent most of the war years there before moving back to Hull firstly to Springhead in January 1945 and then Dairycoates some fifteen months later. In September 1951 and by now numbered 63764, the engine moved into the coal mining area of south Yorkshire and was allocated to Doncaster shed. Mexborough had it from May 1955 until December 1959 when it moved east to Frodingham. After less than a year hauling steel trains, the 2-8-0 went back to coal haulage in November 1960 but this time from Retford depot. In March 1963, after being made redundant by diesel locomotives taking over the workings of the Nottinghamshire coal traffic, No.63764 moved back to Doncaster shed and further employment. The fact that it had undergone a general overhaul less than a year prior to that move must have had a bearing with its ongoing survival. Except for one carried out at Darlington in 1930, all the locomotive's overhauls were undertaken at Gorton works, the ancestral home of the O4s. In this view the engine is looking slightly rundown but it was obviously still running sweetly otherwise condemnation would have occurred in this period when any steam locomotive, no matter what age, was withdrawn for the slightest reason. Remember that by now, October 1965, the Eastern Region based BR Standard 9F 2-10-0's had all but gone for scrap and most of those had not reached double figures in their ages. Note the three welded patches on the bottom half of the smokebox door, no doubt applied with TLC by men who were trying to keep this workhorse in service as long as possible although some of the chalked graffiti would have us believe otherwise. The inevitable took place on Sunday 27th February 1966 and 63764 was withdrawn from service. Less than two months later its cold hulk was purchased for scrap and it finished its days at the Beighton scrapyard of T.W.Ward just a few months past its forty-eighth birthday - value for money or what?

The former Great Northern Railway engine shed on Doncaster Carr had an association with the War Department 2-8-0 from 1943, when hundreds of the eventual 935 built were loaned to the LNER, until steam was banished from the depot in May 1966. This was the scene outside the shed on Sunday 10th October 1965 when the type dominated the allocation and the 'namers' were all but gone. On the right is 90073, one of the original LNER purchased WD's, which had joined the Doncaster allocation in April 1963 after spending much of its life in the East Midlands. No.90305 was one of the batch bought by British Railways which had also spent much of its life working on former LNER lines. Both these engines were withdrawn during the first quarter of 1966 and ended up in Yorkshire scrap yards. Considering that some 733 of these Austerity 2-8-0 types worked for British Railways - in the main being flogged in heavy freight service day in and day out - it is both surprising and somewhat disappointing that none were ever considered for preservation. The speed of their demise is another source of wonderment, one minute there appeared to be hundreds of them slogging away on coal trains, etc., the next minute they had disappeared forever.

Both Crewe and Doncaster shared the maintenance responsibilities for the 'Britannia' class, Doncaster looking after the Eastern Region allocation. On 16th December 1961, No.70008 BLACK PRINCE has just completed a 'General' overhaul and is ready to return home to Norwich Thorpe shed, however, that was not to be the case because a reallocation was to send the Pacific to March and that 32A shedplate was surplus to the engine's requirements. By the end of December 1963 the Eastern Region had got rid of its 'Brits' and 70008 went to Carlisle Kingmoor where, with most of the class following, it managed to keep going until January 1967. As can be seen a fresh coat of paint adorns the locomotive and its tender, probably its last before withdrawal. No.70008 was sold to a Scottish scrapyard a few months after condemnation - age 16 years!

The BR Standard Class 5 was basically a copy of the LMS Stanier version, with a few refinements. Like its predecessor it was a good locomotive and could be found on all the regions of British Railways after its introduction. No.73024 had started life in November 1951 working from Patricroft shed but two years later it went to the Western Region working initially from the WR shed at Chester and then from Canton in Cardiff. At the time of my visit to Doncaster works in December 1961 the 'Standard 5' was working from 89A Shrewsbury depot and by now was entitled to WR fully lined green livery. From Shrewsbury the 4-6-0 moved on to Barrow Road shed in Bristol during July 1962 then three months later it went to another former Midland Railway depot at Gloucester Barnwood. Early in 1963 it was back at Shrewsbury for a six month stint before going to Llanelly of all places where it resided until June 1964 when it was recalled to Barrow Road. Its final depot was Oxford. Considering the relative youth of the class, No.73024 was one of the early withdrawals, succumbing in November 1964 after a two month residence in the university city. It was cut up by J.Buttigieg at Newport in 1965.

In the days before 60103 FLYING SCOTSMAN became really famous, when it was just relatively famous, it carried on with life as the Eastern Region authorities saw fit. During the last week of November and the first couple of weeks of December 1961, whilst undergoing a 'Casual Light' repair at Doncaster, it was fitted with these Witte type smoke deflectors. Nearly all the other extant A3's at that time had them fitted too for safety reasons. At first the German type deflectors brought sounds of ridicule from the railway enthusiast but within a short time people mellowed to them and accepted them - so much so that in its preserved form FLYING SCOTSMAN is once again wearing them, albeit for safety reasons. However, back to Doncaster works in December 1961. No.60103 will shortly be returning to its home depot at King's Cross, after a slight clean and a lick of paint on the new appendages (rust red here but the film is unable to portray that fully). In June of the following year it will return to 'The Plant' for its last 'General' overhaul which will see it back on the main line in July. Six months later it was withdrawn and sold to Alan Pegler whereupon it began a new course in history. This picture was incidentally one of my first and was taken with a borrowed Kodak Brownie.

When it wasn't performing for the crowds, FLYING SCOTSMAN resided on one of the roads in Doncaster engine shed. On Sunday, 10th October 1965 (no specials that day) it catches the last of the afternoon sunlight on its front end. The Pacific has been restored, non-LNER appendages (except the AWS) have been removed, it is repainted and renumbered but it never retired. There is no doubt about it, this locomotive has had an extraordinary life since January 1963. If fiction had followed that same course as the fact then, people would exclaim 'rubbish!' In October 1965 everything was still yet to happen. Oh! and thanks Mr Pegler for saving this beauty from the scrapyard.

Although creating some interest from observers on the Up platform, myself included, O4 Part 8 No.63818 does not appear to be having the same affect with those on the Down platform. The place is the north end of Doncaster station and the date is Saturday 2nd May 1964. The 36A Doncaster based O4 is taking advantage of a lull in the frequency of the express passenger traffic and is using the Up fast to traverse the station with a Sheffield bound coal train. Another ex Ministry of Munitions engine, this O4 became LNER property in December 1923 and was one of the more expensive examples purchased, its cost being some £2,000! Numbered 6264 by Gorton works, the engine went into traffic at Gorton shed during the following February after a 'light' repair. A few months later it moved to the East Midlands and worked from various depots there including Annesley, Colwick, Grantham and New England. Towards the end of World War Two No.6264 moved to Doncaster shed thence to Immingham followed by Frodingham in May 1946. It was whilst allocated to the Scunthorpe shed and by now renumbered to 3818, that Gorton works rebuilt the engine in 1947 to the Part 8 design wherein it got a 5ft 6in. diameter Diagram 100A boiler with round top firebox, new smokebox and a new cab complete with side windows. Staying at Frodingham until July 1958, No.63818 moved to Retford for four and half years before reallocating to Doncaster, its last depot. Withdrawn 17th April 1966, the O4 was amongst the last examples of Eastern Region steam. The following month it was purchased by a Wath based scrap metal merchant and by summer had ceased to exist.

(opposite, top) J50 No.68961 aka Departmental No.14. Condemned 19th September 1965, this is how the 0-6-0 appeared twenty-one days later during a visit I made to the 'Plant' in October. Residing on a track near the scrapyard, the engine is looking rested rather than withdrawn although the chimney is in need of attention. The J50 came to Doncaster from New England shed in June 1962 as No.68961 and after a thirty-six year long career which had been mostly spent working from Bradford Hammerton Street shed. Prior to having a nine year spell at Hornsey shed, from September 1952 to July 1961, the J50 undertook a two year residence at Doncaster shed. New England had it for nearly a year after the sojourn in London but the Peterborough depot had no use for it and sent it Doncaster. Note the Hornsey 34B shedplate still adorning the smokebox door - I wonder if that went to the scrap merchant or was it 'salvaged' beforehand? - a sign of the early 1960's when nobody on the Eastern Region seemed to care much about such trivia as changing shedplates. Although the cast iron 34B is still in place, the brass Doncaster works plates have disappeared, most probably for their metal content and scrap value rather than for nostalgic reasons. Behind the engine is the open ground used when Doncaster works was cutting up hundreds of steam locomotives over the period when that form of traction still ruled. The scrapping of locomotives ceased here in 1964 after some famous locomotives had been demolished including many LNER Pacifics, the Garratt, most of the K3's, and a lot of others including former LMS types. The place was a hive of activity during the period from 1960 to 1963 the likes of which will never be seen again.

(opposite, bottom) Along with six other J50 Departmentals, Nos.10, 11, 12, 13, 15 and 16, all withdrawn May 1965 from Doncaster works, No.14 undertook the short journey to T.W.Ward's scrapyard at Beighton, Sheffield where scrapping took place. It is interesting to note that the J50's pressed into Departmental service were also designated as Stationary Boilers, No.14 for instance became S.B.4525 in September in 1962 on the day it entered Service Stock. Whether the locomotive ever carried out S.B. duties is unknown and from its appearance here there is nothing to indicate that it had been a stationary boiler. For the record, Departmental No.10 (68911) was also S.B.1175; No.11 (68914) - S.B.1176; No.12 (68917) - S.B.4523; No.13 (68929) - S.B.4524; No.15 (68971) - S.B.4526; No.16 (68976) - S.B.4527. Doncaster works, 10th October 1965.

(opposite) **With its nameplates still in situ but with a thick layer of grime removing any title of 'glamorous', 'Jubilee' No.45564 NEW SOUTH WALES hammers through Dore & Totley station with a Leeds (City) to London (St Pancras) express on Saturday 4th April 1964. The fireman leans out of the cab window possibly looking for a response to the smokescreen he has helped create and which looks as good now as it did then. The Holbeck based engine did not have much of a future left. In July it was reallocated to Newton Heath but if it ever got there is unknown because it was withdrawn during the same month. By the end of the year it was pure history having been cut up at Cashmores Great Bridge yard.**

Earlier that day I caught Thompson B1 No.61372 setting off from Dore & Totley with a stopping train from Sheffield (Midland) to Manchester (Central). Having just slipped slightly on the greasy rails the Canklow based B1 gets a grip of its lightly loaded 4-coach train and sets off towards Totley tunnel which on this damp day will not be a pleasant experience for the footplate crew. One of the BR period B1's, coming into traffic as late as December 1950, No.61372 had gone to Immingham shed initially for just ten months and then had spent much of the 50's working on the former Great Eastern Lines from Stratford and later Parkeston depots. Returning north in November 1960, the engine transferred to Darnall shed but moved to Canklow in June 1963. Finally, in a last desperate effort to find suitable work, it moved to Langwith Junction on Sunday 13th June 1965 but was condemned a week later and sold within weeks to T.W.Ward, ending up in their Beighton yard.

Sheep Pasture - the name conjures up thoughts of all kinds of idyllic rural landscapes. In reality, the place was certainly rural and now that all the railway facilities have gone it is probably an idyll but in February 1965 the location was still part of a working railway and had an industrial landscape feel about it, even up here in the middle of Derbyshire hundreds of feet above sea level. There used to be an engine shed here to house the tank engine working this section of the Cromford & High Peak Railway, but it was blown down in a gale shortly before my visit although its small and somewhat decrepit brick bund wall was still in situ. The shed was a timber framed affair, clad in corrugated iron and was probably ready to fall down anyway - the high winds just delivered the finishing blow. Behind the 0-4-0ST is the engine and boiler house for the rope worked incline. To the right of the locomotive is a 'grounded' brake van which was in use as a mess room, although it might be better described by removing the word 'room'. The saddletank, which was stabled for the weekend and also in steam, was one of the four built in 1953 at Horwich, although the design itself dates to the early 1930's.

From this aspect we can see the two water tenders parked behind the 0-4-0ST. These vehicles were necessary for bringing water supplies to Sheep Pasture from the lower sections of the C&HPR and were wound up as required. The locomotives working this section, and which were allocated latterly to Rowsley shed, were changed about once a month or whenever maintenance was needed. No.47006 arrived on the C&HP in November 1963 after a disappointing ten years existence since being built. It first shed was Birkenhead but it spent the last nine months there stored with no work available for such a specialised little engine. In June 1957 it went to Bangor of all places and they utilised it until November 1958 went it was sent to Chester. After a couple of months at 6A it was again put into store until June 1959 when it was packed off to Widnes shed. When they could not find anything suitable they sent it back to Chester who promptly placed the 0-4-0 back in store until they managed to unload it onto Derby on 21st November 1959. After eighteen months of work at 17A the little tank was placed into store again from January to May 1961. However, some work was found for the engine until the end of the year after which it moved to Hasland. It was returned to Derby forthwith and in May 1962 it was sent to Burton but the brewery railways had enough motive power so it returned once again to Derby in June. By now 'the powers that be' who had ordered the saddletanks in the first place must have been getting desperate to find some suitable employment for 47006. In August 1962 No.47006 was allocated to Coalville shed, for what purpose I'm not sure but shunting coal wagons must have been on the agenda. No matter, within a couple of weeks it was back at Derby who now had over a year in which to ponder its future before coming up with the bright idea of the C&HP. So until withdrawn in August 1966, this little engine enjoyed a somewhat solitary life but at least it was employed. It was sold for scrap to J.Cashmore in December 1966 and cut up in their Great Bridge yard.

Just over a year later, on 6th March 1967, I again visited the Cromford & High Peak Railway and this time captured these scenes at Middleton Top engine shed with resident J94 0-6-0ST No.68006 hiding within the roofless and ramshackle 'structure'. This was at least the second engine shed to stand on the site and it was soon to be the last because closure was imminent. The timber frame with its corrugated iron cladding was similar to the late shed which had stood at Sheep Pasture. However, note the proximity of the building on the right, the north-east corner of which actually sticks into the side of the shed - a most unusual affair. When the shed roof disappeared I do not know but the side walls are nearly ready to join it, only the half buried rail stanchions secured to the frame are making it immovable. The water tender is in a deplorable state but the identification is still fixed on the rear.

What of the resident engine - 68006. This 0-6-0 was by now under the charge of Buxton shed having been passed over from Derby at the end of April 1965. The J94 first came to the C&HP in August 1956 being allocated to Rowsley shed for the purpose. When that shed closed in May 1964 Derby took over maintenance for a year until Buxton then took the reins, however, the C&HP engines were actually allocated to the sub shed at Cromford situated at the bottom of the eastern end of the railway. Built in January 1944 by Hudswell, Clarke & Co., No.1755, this engine became LNER property in August 1946, numbered 8006 and sent initially to Immingham depot. In June 1948 Gorton shed had it for six months before passing it on to Bidston. It resided in Cheshire until called for duties on the C&HP, successfully replacing the former North London Railway 0-6-0 tank engines. Altogether seven different J94's worked the line until closure in 1967. No.68006 was there with the first four, the others being 68013, 68030 and 68034. No.68012 came in 1957 but in 1962 Nos.68030 and 68034 were withdrawn and replaced by 68068 and 68079. Condemned May 1967, No.68006 was sold for scrap to the same firm as 47006 in August. Finally, detail of the shed's architecture is discernible in this view; the stout timber frame is secured to the stanchions with U-bolts and the corrugated iron contrasts vividly with the ornate windows set in the north wall. The corner stonework of the intruding building leaves little clearance. The passing of the Cromford & High Peak in 1967 virtually coincided with the end of steam on BR. That such a railway line could exist for as long as the steam locomotive seems, today, inconceivable given the nature of the route and the traffic passing over it. But, exist it did for about one hundred and forty years.

(right) Here is one of Rowsley shed's more usual fare - the ubiquitous LMS 'Jinty'. This is No.47629 on Saturday 4th April 1964, working the yard alongside the engine shed. Compared with some of the more industrially placed yards on British Railways, Rowsley offered something of the rural idyll although in winter the proximity of buildings does offer some shelter from the weather. This 0-6-0T was one of the last built, being turned out from Beardmore & Co. in 1928 as LMS No.16712. The coal rails on top of the bunker were a later addition and were not unique with many of these engines having different combinations of rails added over the years. No.47629 was one of the longer lasting examples of its class being withdrawn as late as November 1967. It was sold for scrap to a well known yard in Newport, Monmouthshire in 1968.

Langwith Junction shed had one function in life indeed the sole reason for its existence, especially being stuck out in the middle of nowhere, was to serve the local coal mines. Its motive power reflected its workings which consisted moving coal trains and returning the empties. Opened by the Lancashire, Derbyshire & East Coast Railway during the 1890's, the depot at first consisted a two road shed but this was later extended. In 1907 the LD&EC was absorbed into the Great Central Railway and shortly after that event the depot was enlarged by erecting a three road shed alongside the original building. Once that was completed the company brought in more motive power to cope with the growth in coal traffic originating locally. The GC brought in their heavyweight engines for this job, firstly the 0-6-0 tender engines then the 0-8-0 type, rapidly followed by the O4 2-8-0 which remained at the shed until closure. The last of the 0-6-0 type, the Robinson J11 or 'Pom-Poms' as they were nicknamed universally, worked until September 1962 and on 23rd of that month Nos.64314 and 64379 were both condemned and sent to Gorton works for cutting up. Here the pair languish in the shed yard waiting for the tow over and under the Pennines. No.64314 was a relative newcomer to Langwith Junction in the annals of this class and its arrival in March 1957 straight from a General overhaul at Gorton also signified its last visit to works prior to scrapping. Built by Neilson Reid and released to traffic in April 1902, the 0-6-0 went first to Immingham shed where except for a three week residency at Lincoln shed in 1944, it stayed until moving to Langwith - nearly a record perhaps - 55 years at one depot. No.64379 had experienced a much more travelled existence. Built by Vulcan Foundry in August 1904, the engine had three separate associations with Langwith Junction the first being in 1922 which was swiftly followed by a two year stint from September 1925. The final residence started in October 1939. In between those different allocations, No.64379 spent time at Ardsley, Colwick, Frodingham, Immingham, Lincoln, Louth and Neasden. Refreshingly, the tenders have been emptied of coal - perhaps a Gorton memo forbid such practices as leaving coal in a locomotive entering works for any reason.

As late as 30th August 1965 Langwith Junction shed could still present a reasonable show of former LNER motive power. This trio of resident Class O4 Part 8 engines is headed by 63612 with 63739 behind. The third engine is, I'm afraid, unidentified. Though nearing the end of their working lives now, all three of the 2-8-0s were still active but this would be their last summer. No.63612 was withdrawn during November whilst 63739 succumbed earlier at the beginning of October. Langwith Junction engine shed closed in February of the following year, its duties taken on by a new diesel depot sited at nearby Shirebrook. Note the roof of W.H.Davis Wagon Works in the background - this firm is still in business whereas the 'new' diesel depot at Shirebrook is long closed.

The former Midland Railway roundhouse at Barrow Hill in Staveley became one of the last strongholds for steam locomotives in the north Midlands. Add to that the fact that the place had been partially rebuilt as lately as 1958, when a new roof was put on, giving the place a light and airy ambience. It closed to steam on 4th October 1965 but during the previous weekend I paid a visit to photograph the last resident steam locomotives before they were dispersed to other sheds or scrapyards. WD 90573 was already condemned and had been consigned for scrap in August but was yet to depart. Ex-Johnson MR 1F 0-6-0T No.41835 was one of the last five of that class (41708, 41734, 41763 and 41804 were others recently employed) which worked the Staveley works complex via a long standing Agreement between the Midland Railway and the Staveley Iron Company. The 100 year agreement to supply shunting engines did not expire until 1966. Although all of the aforementioned 0-6-0T were still officially in stock at the time of my visit, they were all stored out of use. Behind the 0-6-0T is 0-4-0ST No.47001 which had, at last, found some decent work (at the iron company) after years of unemployment. The saddletank had started life at Edge Hill shed in December 1932 and in November 1946 moved 'on loan' to nearby Bank Hall shed, a transfer made permanent the following month. However, from August 1952 until April 1963 this little 0-4-0 was stored in a serviceable condition on no less than thirty-nine occasions - something of a record perhaps? In May 1963 it was transferred to Agecroft but that shed sent it on to Barrow Hill a month later.

(right) **No.47005 was one of the BR Horwich versions of the LMS Kitson 0-4-0 saddletanks. This engine had also arrived at Barrow Hill in June 1963 after a somewhat idle ten years spent at Birkenhead and Preston, with long periods of storage.**

(below) **Outside, in the shed yard and stabled for the weekend with some of Barrow Hill's own WD's, was Westhouses based Stanier 8F No.48149. As can be seen, the weather was hardly suitable for walking about never mind photography, but in between the heavy showers I managed to expose some film (we had in fact just experienced a violent summer thunderstorm and lightning had wrecked one of my negatives). The 8F was just twenty-three years old on this date having been one of the wartime engines delivered to the LMS at Kingmoor depot in August 1942. Within four months it had infiltrated into Scotland and was allocated to Grangemouth shed for the next six years after which it was replaced, by WD 2-8-0 and 2-10-0's, and sent south to Wellingborough. In December 1950 it ended up at Stourton shed and enjoyed nearly ten years there before returning to Wellingborough for a sixteen month stay. Next it was off to Toton for nearly three years, then to Derby in February 1964. Westhouses had only had it a month when I photographed it but they kept hold of it for another year before it moved to Sutton Oak to be amongst its kind. It was withdrawn in January 1967 and sold for scrap.**

Although still officially 'on the books', 0-6-0T No.41804 and its fellow compatriots were looking their age at Barrow Hill during my 26th September 1965 visit. The rain was just starting but there was still some late summer sun to lend good natural light to these subjects. Note the electrification warning flash on the bunker of 41804 which contrasts with the lion and wheel emblem still gracing the tank side nearly ten years after it was superseded. Also in this line were 41763 and 41708. All three engines had their shedplates and worksplates removed but whether this was carried out by shed staff or 'collectors' is unknown. In 1966 all five of the 'Staveley shunters' were officially withdrawn and four of them were sold for scrap No.41708 was purchased for preservation and today resides at the Swanage Railway.

Just about holding on, courtesy of the Staveley Iron job, former Midland four-coupled tank engine No.41528 graces the yard at Barrow Hill in September 1965. This Deeley 0-4-0T was one of two survivors (41533 was the other) still working and wearing the 41E shedplate. How this outside cylinder engine with its complicated Walschaerts valve gear survived this long, when any reason under the sun was being used to condemn steam locomotives, is hard to fathom. Not the most elegant of locomotives, No.41528 managed to see in the New Year at Staveley. For book keeping purposes all the 0-6-0 and 0-4-0 tank engines were transferred to Langwith Junction (41J) engine shed but were actually in store at Canklow (41D) shed and an entry in the April 1966 *Railway Observer* states " Langwith Junction closed to steam from 6th February 1966 and the nine small tank engines from Staveley (stored at Canklow) cannot be condemned until an Agreement of 1866 between the Midland Railway and Staveley Works is repealed."

(opposite) **A visit to Swindon works on Sunday 23rd June 1963 found lots of steam motive power about the place although it was obvious that the diesels were taking over. 'Manor' No.7822 FOXCOTE MANOR was coming to the end of a 'Heavy Intermediate' repair, its last before withdrawal, and was yet to be married up to its tender prior to return to its home shed at Oswestry. Note that the 89D shedplate has yet to be refitted. 7822 went new to Oswestry in December 1950 then four years later went to Chester for a similar time period before returning to Oswestry in August 1958. Its time at Oswestry, indeed that particular depot's association with the Manor class, ended in December 1963 when it moved to Machynlleth along with 7807, 7810 and 7827. Finally, in January 1965 No.7822 made its fateful move to Shrewsbury and immortality.**

Another ex-works locomotive basking in the sunshine at Swindon on that June Sunday in 1963 was 'Grange' No.6847 TIDMARSH GRANGE of 88A Cardiff East Dock. Previously allocated to Canton depot, the 4-6-0 was evicted from that shed during August 1962 to make way for the alterations which would transform Canton into a modern diesel depot. After East Dock, the 'Grange' moved to Ebbw Junction in July 1965 and finally, in the last quarter of that year, it worked from 85A Worcester shed prior to withdrawal. In this picture we can see that No.6847 had just finished a 'General' and has been turned out fully repainted with not a blemish yet spoiling the immaculate finish. Of course, sights such as this would become rarer at Swindon as steam locomotive overhauls began to wind down and in less than two years they would cease completely.

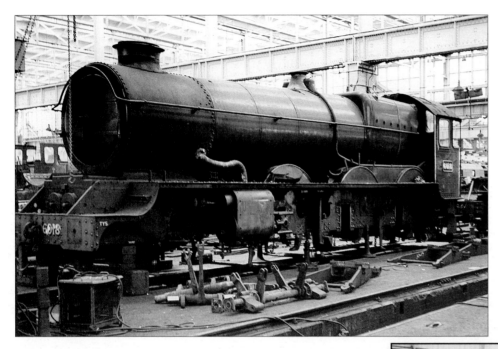

(left) Although withdrawn on the last day of 1962, 'King' No.6018 KING HENRY VI was used a couple of times during 1963 to haul special trains. At the end of April it worked from Tyseley shed on local trains for a couple of days around Birmingham prior to taking out a Stephenson Locomotive Society railtour from Birmingham to Southall, Swindon and return. Prior to its next outing, the apparent 'last King trip' to Birmingham, the engine went through a minor overhaul at Swindon and here on 23rd June 1963 is a photographic record of that event. Once the 1963 special trains were run, the 'King' returned to Swindon and was cut-up in October.

(right) Also in the shops at Swindon in June 1963, shorn of some of its more collectable brasswork, was 'King' No.6000 KING GEORGE V. This engine was scheduled for preservation and housing in Swindon museum but the museum apparently did not have room. Nevertheless, restoration took place and No.6000 resided at Swindon for some years before going on loan to Bulmers Ltd. in 1968 and made ready for main line running. The rest of the engine's life after that is modern history and does not require retelling here.

(opposite) Sticking with the 'Kings' at Swindon in June 1963, I present this nice portrait of No.6025 KING HENRY III in the yard outside 'A' shop. Although minus tender and the more important pieces of brass, the engine is very much intact and appears to be in good condition. Behind is No.6026 KING JOHN in a similar state. Both engines had recently arrived from Old Oak Common shed where they had been in store since their withdrawal in the previous December. The authorities apparently kept these engines 'stored' in case they were required for the 1963 Summer workings in the possible event of diesel locomotive failures. As it turned out they were not needed, hence the call to Swindon for their eventual scrapping.

Swindon works employed a small fleet of 0-6-0 Pannier tank locomotives for the numerous shunting duties that such a large establishment generated. Usually each engine had a Shunters Truck attached which belonged to the Locomotive Department and which was numbered in a regional fleet list. As late as September 1963 the Western Region still employed 265 of these trucks, which were peculiar to the Western, with 45 of them based in the Bristol Division of which four were allocated to Swindon, another 79 were based in the Cardiff Division, 60 more in the London Division and the final 29 in the Plymouth Division. Pannier No.8738 was one of the earlier members of the huge 863 strong class designed by Collett and built between 1929 and 1949. On a visit to Swindon in May 1964 the pair were resting for the weekend but the Pannier was no longer in the Capital Stock list and had been withdrawn for about a year though was still very active. Its last shed had been Neyland but following a trip to Swindon for repair it was withdrawn, though still serviceable, and taken into the work's own shunting fleet. Note the two types of coupling and the obvious, by now, lack of a shedplate on the smokebox door.

(opposite) Still amongst the active list at Swindon works in June 1963 was 'Castle' No.4082 WINDSOR CASTLE of Old Oak Common shed. Although shunted into a dead-end siding with a 16-ton mineral wagon, six-wheel milk tank and a couple of tenders for company, the engine was due for repair and afterwards would continue in service for another year. In August 1964 No.4082 transferred to Gloucester Horton Road shed but it was only there for a short period before being condemned. This was the 'Castle' which was originally numbered 7013, carried the name BRISTOL CASTLE and changed identities with the original locomotive in February 1952 because the real 4082 was mechanically unsuitable to draw the funeral train of the late King George VI. Once the change was made, the identities did not revert back.

Swindon engine shed 26th June 1963. Two of Hawksworth's 'Modified Halls', No.6961 STEDHAM HALL and 6974 BRYNGWYN HALL, both from Old Oak Common shed, grace the seemingly quiet yard. From this aspect the shed appeared to be a straight road, dead-end affair made up of a central five road section, with a two road section on each side but at the rear and also on the east (right) side were two adjacent square roundhouses. The three sheds dated from different periods with the straight shed opening in 1871, the rear (north) roundhouse in 1892 and the east building opening in 1908. By the summer of 1963 the whole lot were rundown and in need of repair or replacement but that was not to be and, after closure in 1964, the whole site was eventually demolished. Note the dead-end siding of the elevated coal stage on the left, a good vantage point for photographing motive power on the shed yard or trains on the Gloucester main line.

(opposite) Tucked in behind 6974 was 'Grange' No.6851 HURST GRANGE, of Wolverhampton Oxley shed, another 4-6-0 which had just completed a 'General' at the works. The overhaul will see the engine through another two years work prior to withdrawal. The coal in the tender is some of the best we have seen so far, obviously Swindon liked to give its charges' a 'good send off' at the completion of repairs. Visible on the right is the high pitched roof of the 'new' 1908 built roundhouse.

Just inside the straight shed at Swindon depot was an Old Oak Common based BR Standard 9F, No.92243. This was one of the Crewe built 2-10-0's and came into traffic in October 1958 at Ebbw Junction shed in Newport. At the end of the 1963 Summer Timetable it would return to Wales, this time being allocated to Cardiff East Dock shed. Severn Tunnel Junction shed also had its services for a couple of months in 1964 but by then suitable work was hard to find for these excellent locomotives. In October 1965 it went to Barrow Road shed in Bristol then, when that shed closed, it moved on to Bath Green Park but probably never turned a wheel there in revenue service because it was withdrawn during December, just seven years old! Five months later it was back in South Wales at the Newport scrapyard of J.Cashmore. Finally on this picture, note the lone light bulb hanging just above the right hand smoke deflector of 92243 - surreal or what?

Further into the shed, behind the 9F was this Swindon based 'County', No.1012 COUNTY OF DENBIGH, which was turned out in a reasonable condition but was only months away from withdrawal. No doubt about it, the days of the steam locomotive on BR was rapidly diminishing and I had to make a concerted effort to record as much as possible on film. Luckily this was not to be my last trip to Swindon but on each successive visit I noticed the changes. Behind the Pannier tank can be seen the turntable of the 1892 roundhouse with a number of diesel shunters already in residence and taking up the stalls. Note the curvature of the smoke troughs over the tracks which led directly from the straight shed to the roundhouse.

(above and opposite) **Less than one year on and I am back at Swindon shed, again courtesy of the RCTS East Midlands branch and their 'Duchess' hauled** *THE EAST MIDLANDER*. **The date was 9th May, the weather was reasonable and this is the view of the shed yard from the coaling stage. Stealing centre stage and looking thoroughly 'at home', is our motive power for the trip in the appropriate shape of 46251 CITY OF NOTTINGHAM. The Pacific had arrived from Crewe in this sparkling condition and had spent the Friday night on Annesley shed - what a superb job Crewe had done. It was a shame that 46251 was withdrawn at the end of that summer and then sold for scrap. Alongside the 'Duchess' is 'Castle' No.7022 HEREFORD CASTLE which, as will be noted, was nothing like as clean although the driver is making sure that the oil reservoirs are topped up. The 'Castle' was a standby engine for the** *CASTLE FAREWELL* **trips run by the Western Region from Paddington to Plymouth on the same day. As can be seen, the diesels, both electric and hydraulic types, are muscling-in - the WR made a determined effort to banish steam from its main lines before any of the other regions managed it. On the subject of 46251 with a railtour from Nottingham, the outspoken East Midlands Branch Hon. Sec. Vic Forster, obviously in conversation with a Western Region enthusiast, was overheard to say " When we take an engine on a railtour we bring the same B****** engine back with us !!"**

One year and twenty days later - 29th May 1965 - and 'foreign' motive power once again graces the yard at Swindon shed by dint of the RCTS East Midlands branch. However, this time we had something of a disaster on our hands because the engine which had brought us from Nottingham, the preserved A3 No.4472 FLYING SCOTSMAN, had suffered a broken tender spring. Alan Pegler (in the cap) and his fitter are surveying the damage. It worked out that a plate within the spring had broken and it was duly repaired by clamping it together. No.4472 returned to Nottingham via the Lickey incline, subject to a speed restriction of 60 m.p.h. Apparently a certain Nottingham based gentleman arrived back in the city with a big grin on his face. It will be noticed that the Swindon coaling stage is now all but redundant its massive, Gothic like, architecture was soon to be razed.

24th October 1964 signified the last A4 working from King's Cross, a joint endeavour between the RCTS and the Stephenson Locomotive Society - *THE JUBILEE REQUIEM* 1964. Here at Peascliffe, on a cold but clear morning, No.60009 UNION OF SOUTH AFRICA seems to be making easy work of the job in hand. By now based at Ferryhill shed in Aberdeen, the A4 continued working until June 1966 and was then, happily, purchased for preservation. Notice the immaculate state of the trackwork on this section of the ECML.

During the RCTS East Midlander No.6 railtour to Crewe and Horwich in October 1963, the motive power, 'Crab' No.42896, stopped at Lichfield Trent valley High Level to top up its tender with water. This gave many of us travelling on the train the opportunity to grab a quick shot of the engine prior to getting under way. The early morning autumn sunshine was bathing the train in its warm rays but the 'Crab' was busy making steam and blowing off in the process thereby casting a shadow over itself. Nevertheless, I think that the result is worth while, with plenty of contrast between the shiny and shady highly polished paintwork of the engine. Note the Cafeteria coach behind the engine - snacks on tap all day. This coach, or at least half of it was usually the abode of the RCTS top brass. Next stop Crewe.

On a gloriously sunny, and warm, Saturday 18th April 1964, A3 No.60051 BLINK BONNY was used for a railtour from Sowerby Bridge via Derby to Crewe and is seen here heading westwards at Willington, taking the former North Staffordshire line to Stoke-on-Trent via Uttoxeter. The six-coach formation of BR Mk.1 coaches was an easy load for the Pacific although the route was somewhat strange and the A3 must have been one of the first ex-LNER Pacifics to have gone that way. Allocated to Gateshead shed at the time, 60051 was looking exceedingly clean for a Tyneside based steam locomotive, the depot having a somewhat dubious reputation in BR days for having a lack of cleaners although their fitters did an excellent job keeping their engines a fine mechanical condition during the latter months of steam working from the shed. For the record 60051 had spent the night prior to this railtour stabled at Hillhouse shed in Huddersfield. Withdrawn in November 1964, BLINK BONNY was sold for scrap to Hughes, Bolckow at North Blyth in January 1965.

Health & Safety Exec. Eat your heart out! or more likely throw a wobbly. This scene at the closed station known as Melton Mowbray (North) took place on Saturday 18th May 1963 when the RCTS East Midlands branch railtour reached that place via the GN&LNW Joint line from Bottesford West Junction. The railtour took in many of the closed or about to close branches in the counties of Nottinghamshire, Leicestershire and Rutland including the Cottesmore branch, the line to Leicester (Belgrave Road), plus the Uppingham branch. Melton Mowbray (North) was still a centre for goods traffic and through traffic from Northampton and Leicester GN to Nottingham and Colwick yard, however, the crowds of enthusiasts seem to be unaware of any dangers which might have been forthcoming as they straddle the track on the bridge over Scalford Road. The motive power for the eight coach train throughout the day consisted Stanier Cl.5 No.45238, supplied by Nottingham shed, Cl.4 tank No.42087 and Cl.4F No.44414 which both came from Leicester Midland shed and were nicely turned out by that depot. Whilst the Cl.5 was taking water, the crowds streamed off the train and as can be seen got basically into every nook and cranny it was possible to fill. The station platform had probably never seen as many passengers in all the years it was open.

At Market Harborough the 2-6-4T took over at the rear of the train. Note the reporting number now changed from 1X28 to 1X40. We got to this latter place via Belgrave Road terminus where No.45238 ran round the train, coupled onto the rear and ran tender first to John O'Gaunt where the Class 5 ran round again and continued over the Joint Line to Market Harborough. At Leicester the enthusiasts again clambered all over the infrastructure of the terminus, even climbing onto signal posts. - a free for all it seemed as everyone vied to get the best photographic positions. Later the 4F and 42087 took the train over the Uppingham branch and at that station the crowds once again trod the trackwork. Apparently, that RCTS special was the last passenger train to use the branch.

At Luffenham the Class 4 tank and the Class 5 take water before taking the special to visit the Cottesmore Ironstone branch. The 2-6-4T was one of those built to work on the Southern Region and started its operational life at Newhaven in March 1951. A year later it went to Brighton and after four years there moved on to Tunbridge Wells West shed. Stewarts Lane got it in September 1956 and kept hold of it until June 1959 when it moved, temporarily, back to Tunbridge Wells for six months when it moved over to the Midland Region at Neasden. Cricklewood got it next, but only from June to September 1962 when Leicester Midland shed claimed it. Moving further north in May 1964, No.42087 went to Bolton for a month prior to settling down at Newton Heath in June. Birkenhead was its last shed and it was withdrawn from there in October 1966, just fifteen and a half years old. Since it went new to Chester shed in August 1936, the Class 5 had served at no less than seventeen sheds on the Western, Midland and Central divisions of the former LMS. It finished up not far from where it started, at Warrington Dallam. It was withdrawn in December 1966 and was sold for scrap.

This is the scene at Manton station in the late afternoon of that May Saturday. By now most of the people on board the train were relaxing in anticipation of the final leg of the tour. The sun rays are bathing the engines whilst three BR officials chat. Our train is waiting for a Kettering-Nottingham 'stopper' from the Corby line to pass and clear the section before setting off north. We left there some 21 minutes late. No.42087, top and tailed with 45238, took us over the Cottesmore branch after which 45238 provided our motive power back to Nottingham. What a glorious day that was - all courtesy of the RTCS.

One thing about the East Midlands branch of the Railway Correspondence & Travel Society, whenever they organised rail tours they certainly did it in style. Besides the motive power, we had some excellent clean coaching stock with carriage boards adorning most of them. *(above)* The 9th May 1964 trip, to Eastleigh and Swindon, had the appropriately named 'Duchess' at the head and here on the outward leg we stopped at Rugby (Central) for water. I took advantage of the fact that there was no traffic in the Up siding to capture the sunny side of the train. Note the numerous heads sticking out of the carriage windows. *(opposite)* The 29th May 1965 'bash' went out to Swindon by a different route than the one taken by 46251. Here at Wellingborough we are stopped to take on water, and for a chance of a couple of photographs besides inspection of FLYING SCOTSMAN. There are a large number of visible faces on this shot and though I cannot put a name to all of them, I can pick out John Henton, Dave Reynolds and Harold Miller.

(*above*) **Platform 5, Leicester (Central), Saturday 29th August 1964.** The Poole to Bradford train is awaiting the 'off' signal to continue its northbound journey. The train engine, though nothing to write home about in the cleanliness stakes, was Oxley based ex Great Western 'Hall' No.6925 HACKNESS HALL, a regular performer on this train. The 'Hall' will take the train to its next stop at Nottingham (Victoria) where it will be relieved usually by a 'Jubilee'. The Western Region engines were then turned on the Bagthorpe-Basford North-Bulwell Common triangle ('Round the handle') went back light engine southwards from whence they came. One however, tried to turn on the south end turntable at Nottingham Vic and fell backwards into the pit. I went especially to Leicester for a ride back behind this one.

(above) **Standing in for the regular motive power which had no doubt failed, BR Standard 9F No.92154 gets ready to depart Leicester (Central) with the York-Bournemouth 'express' on 29th August 1964. The Annesley 9F's were regular performers on GC main line express passenger trains and their exploits became legendary, especially regarding the high speeds they attained. No.92154 was a relative newcomer to the large Annesley fleet, arriving at the shed in February, although it had spent four months there in 1958. In July 1965, along with the remaining 2-10-0's still allocated - 1965 saw the Annesley fleet dispersed to all corners - 92154 left the depot and moved to Kirkby-in-Ashfield for a few days before settling at Speke Junction shed for its remaining two years of operational life. Note Leicester's own station turntable tucked away on the right behind the horse dock.**

(opposite, bottom) **The station pilot on this summer Saturday was Stanier 8F No.48079 from Annesley shed. Throughout its 30-year career, this freight locomotive had certainly had a colourful life. Starting at Toton in December 1936, it joined the Army in October 1942, was numbered WD.602 and in July 1943 was demobbed back to the LMS but at Motherwell shed from where it worked until June 1946 when it went south to Kingmoor. Five months later it was resident at Royston shed hauling Yorkshire coal for a living. During the first April of the BR period it reallocated to Derby and spent the next thirteen years there. In March 1961 it started an eighteen month stint at Kettering prior to moving to Annesley in September of the following year. The Nottinghamshire depot kept hold 48079 until June 1965 when Toton got it back for a couple of weeks. Lostock Hall was its next depot but only for four months before moving to Lancaster. Spending the winter at Green Ayre shed the 2-8-0 returned to Lostock Hall during the following April but its tenure there was short lived and it went to its final shed, Rose Grove, in July. Withdrawn in December, it was sold for scrap to Draper's in Hull in June 1967. Note that some wag had placed a 'Gentlemen' toilet sign just above the cab windows.**

Annesley's brief flirtation with the 'Royal Scot's' was over by June 1965 and Stanier Class 5's had taken over most of the depot's passenger turns including the Nottingham-Marylebone semi-fasts. However, on 28th June 1965, the 2-38 p.m. ex-Marylebone (I was travelling back on this train and jumped off for a quick shot of the engine) was hauled into Leicester (Central) by a Crewe South Cl.5 No.45128 which must have either been on loan or had been seconded somewhere along the line. Anyway, here it is for all to see. It must have got back to Crewe at some time shortly afterwards because it was transferred to Springs Branch shed in July. It worked out its remaining days in Lancashire being withdrawn in September 1966 and was then sold for scrap.

On Sunday 11th November 1962 I ventured over to Stoke-on-Trent and was pleasantly surprised by the number of 4F's still gracing the shed, with twenty-eight still on the books. No.44271 was in service and resting for the weekend amongst the other assorted motive power, whereas 44393 had just been withdrawn.

Over in the roofless ex-North Staffordshire Railway roundhouse, situated on the west side of the main line, was No.44307 which had been withdrawn in October. Though separated from its tender, the 4F would soon be on its way to Cashmores at Great Bridge for scrapping.

(opposite) It was to be nearly two years before I returned to Stoke to photograph the steam power. Resting on the Down through line, prior to setting off for home on Wednesday 12th August 1964, was Warrington Dallam 8F No.48500 with a mixed freight in tow. Electrification was just about to engulf this former NSR route between Manchester (Piccadilly - London Road) and London (Euston) and luckily the station kept its overall roof during that event.

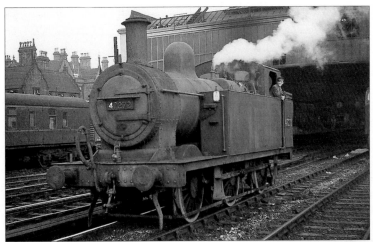

Knocking about the station on pilot duties on that Wednesday in 1964 was one of the once numerous LMS 'Jinty' 0-6-0 tanks, No.47272. Hardly looking its best, the engine was nevertheless busy and would remain so until withdrawn in June two years hence.

(below) Back inside the old NSR roundhouse at Stoke, 27th March 1966. This Ivatt 2-6-0, No.43002 has just been transferred to 5D from Bescot hence the lack of shedplate. As far as the absent front numberplate is concerned, I can only assume that whoever was given the instruction at Bescot to 'take the plate off the smokebox door' did exactly that but because they were not sure which plate should be removed, they removed both. That is my theory as I shudder to think that some enthusiast might have taken it during the hours of darkness. No.43002 was one of the original LMS built Cl.4's, coming out of Horwich in December 1947 and being allocated to Crewe South shed. During the first month of Nationalisation the engine transferred to Bletchley where it resided until September 1953. Nuneaton then got it and kept hold of it for the next nine years until a move to Bescot was authorised in October 1962. Stoke used the engine from March 1966 until August 1967 when No.43002 moved on to Workington where four months after its arrival there, the mogul was withdrawn and sold for scrap.

By March 1966 the infrastructure concerning the servicing and maintenance of steam locomotives was either redundant, non-existent or badly run down. The ash plant at Stoke just got into the latter category but if it held on until the depot closed in August 1967 I do not know. Erected by the LMS in the mid 1930's, as part of the engine shed improvement programme which was being carried out system wide, this ash plant was unique on that railway and possibly throughout the country. The neighbouring coaling plant was of a standard design (No.2) adopted by the LMS. Spanning three tracks, the ash plant serviced two of them by hoisting the moveable ash skip over to the stationary wagon (seen on the right) and tipping the contents. Having just topped up its tender at the coaling plant, Cl.5 No.45268 is now having its fire cleaned out and is positioned as such that the skip receiving its clinker would be directly beneath the hoist although it did not matter where the locomotive was positioned because the skips in the pit were mobile. However, after thirty years of constant use and very little maintenance of late, the tracks on which the skips ran were in a sorry state. What of 45268 which on this day was looking rather splendid. The engine had transferred to Stoke in April 1964 from Saltley where it had been allocated since new in October 1936. In May 1967, shortly before Stoke shed closed, No.45268 moved on to the relative safety of Lancashire where the last of BR steam were assembling for the final act. It went first to Springs Branch, then in December to Newton Heath. In July 1968 it was sent to Carnforth where, during the following month, it became one of the last working British Railways steam locomotives.

In the event of an express locomotive failure on any part of the East Coast Main Line, 'main line pilots' (usually a Pacific) were positioned at the more important centres along the entire route. Peterborough, Grantham, Doncaster, York, Darlington, Newcastle and Tweedmouth all had them. Something of an extravagance the accountants might say today. Not in the least, because a failure on the main line was soon cleared and inconvenience was kept to a minimum for all concerned - not just the fare paying public but also the goods, coal, livestock and mail trains travelling behind. Basically the system did not snarl up as is often the case today. On 1st June 1963 *(above)* A3 No.60106 FLYING FOX suffered a hot middle big-end just north of Peterborough whilst working a Newcastle - King's Cross express. The A3 had only just taken over the train at Grantham so the problem had soon manifested itself. Here, at around midday, the filthy engine limped into Peterborough ready for the stop. *(opposite)* Uncoupled and released a few minutes later, 60106 was shunted into the Up bay platform road so that New England based Thompson A2/3 No.60520 could carry out its main line pilot duty and take the train on to King's Cross. Ironically the A3 was given a Casual Light repair at Doncaster works and remained operational for another eighteen months whereas the A2 was withdrawn sixteen days later and then summoned to the same establishment at the end of August and cut-up.

(above) **Covering for a diesel failure, King's Cross based A4 No.60032 GANNET exits Peterborough with a northbound express on 1st June 1963. Looking far from the usually immaculate Top Shed turn-out, the A4 was working out its last months and by the end of the year it would be called into Doncaster and scrapped. Note the coal stacked high in the corridor tender, hardly any has been shovelled onto the fire yet.** *(opposite)* **Having just run under Spital bridge 60032 starts to accelerate away from the station towards New England where the busy yards appear to belie the fact that goods services on BR were in a rapid decline. This was the last year of Pacific working on the ECML and I was making the best of it when the weather forecast allowed.**

Earlier in the day steam workings were frequent enough to warrant me staking a pitch at the north end of the station and in this view of a King's Cross-Leeds (Central) express, York based A1 No.60126 starts away without a breath of smoke. Many of the Leeds services were diagrammed for 'Deltic' haulage by now but the mysteries of the complicated diesel engines were still creating problems for the authorities and so good old reliable steam (60106 apart) was still holding its own.

Shortly afterwards, King's Cross A4 No.60034 LORD FARRINGDON enters from the north whilst the Station Inspector checks the road before making his way across the tracks to the island platform. 60034 was one of the longer lived A4's and took up residence at New England sixteen days after this encounter. By the end of October it had moved off to St Margarets shed for the winter before allocating to Aberdeen Ferryhill for a two year stint on the Aberdeen-Glasgow 3-hour expresses. Note the mixture of BR Mark 1 and LNER Gresley rolling stock of the London bound train.

Round about lunchtime I moved to the south end of Peterborough station to get a different aspect and capture the light. This is 60021 WILD SWAN about to depart for King's Cross but soon to join the other 'Top Shed' A4's later that month at New England. The day had turned out superbly. Plenty of steam, many of the expresses Pacific hauled and a little bit of drama to top it off. What more could one ask for at such a late date in the age of steam on the ECML.

(opposite) Another heavy southbound, this time from Leeds, with Copley Hill A1 No.60120 KITTIWAKE at the helm. By the end of the Summer Timetable this engine was surplus at 56C and moved to York where, shortly after Christmas it was laid up and then withdrawn. It entered Darlington works for scrapping at the end of January less than fourteen years after coming into traffic for British Railways.

One week later - 8th June 1963 - and with another superb sunny Saturday to gladden the heart, my friend and I drove over to the ECML but this time I fancied some main line speed to practice my panning skills so the obvious place was the south end of Stoke tunnel where, in early afternoon especially, the sun shone into the deep cutting enough to light up the west side of both Up and Down trains. Once again I was blessed with lots of steam power but mainly in the shape of A3's. First out of the tunnel was 60044 MELTON with the *ANGLO SCOTTISH CAR CARRIER*. Running well and with a heavy load, it is hard to believe, even now, that just one week later this engine was condemned at King's Cross shed and by the end of the year ceased to exist after being broken up at Doncaster works.

With eleven on A3 No.60065 KNIGHT OF THISTLE speeds northwards towards the tunnel mouth in excellent sunshine. This New England based A3 was, like 60044, another of the A3's rebuilt from A1/A10. The following weekend No.60065 was reallocated to Grantham shed to make way for the influx of Pacifics being moved from King's Cross to New England, however, it was back in Peterborough in late October and continued working from that depot through the winter. Condemned at the end of June 1964, the A3 was sold for scrap to Norwich merchant R.A.King.

(opposite, top) **On Friday 7th September 1962, in a bid to sharpen my camera skills on some moving subjects, I journeyed the short distance from home in Nottingham to Grantham where the East Coast Pacifics beckoned. First in view was A4 No.60030 GOLDEN FLEECE which was coming off shed ready to take over a London bound train. The engine was looking slightly cleaner than it had been when I last saw it in December but it had just been released from Doncaster works after spending most of August in there receiving a 'Casual Light' overhaul, its last as things turned because in December King's Cross 'Top Shed' was having a clear-out and 60030, along with 60003, 60014, 60028 and 60033 were doomed - the first of the A4's to be scrapped.**

(opposite, bottom) **Another Pacific coming off shed was A3 No.60054 PRINCE OF WALES but it was ready to work a northbound express. One of the early rebuilds from A1 class, this engine had been allocated to Grantham shed since June 1957 performing such duties and could be seen the length and breadth of the ECML. Shortly after British Railways came into existence, and long before it was fitted with the smoke deflectors, it had a long seven and a half years stretch working on the former Great Central main line and was allocated to Leicester shed for that purpose. Back to the 1960's, this engine was affected by the closure of Grantham shed inasmuch as being moved to Doncaster shed then, like other Grantham A3's which survived the moves, ending up in Norwich for scrapping.**

(this page) **Newly arrived at Grantham shed from New England in June, V2 No.60948 makes its way through the station ready for a southbound working. The engine's stay at Grantham was short-lived as it returned to New England at the end of November. With the influx of engines to New England from the closed 'Top Shed' in June 1963, the V2 went to Doncaster shed but was condemned at the end of the Summer Timetable workings. It joined the ranks of the fifty-five V2's which were eventually cut-up at Doncaster works.**

(*above*) **Tuesday 16th April 1963 was a day with a rather damp start but having committed myself to a day at Grantham there was no turning back. Luckily, and true to the monthly prediction, the rain came as showers. My first shot of the day was of Ardsley based A3 No.60036 COLOMBO heading this heavy southbound express from Leeds with apparent ease. One of the original A3's, 60036 managed a thirty year life before withdrawal in November 1964 and during that time it had been allocated to most of the depots on the ECML in England except Grantham and New England. Built and later scrapped in Yorkshire, the engine had spent some eighteen years of its life working from sheds in Yorkshire.**

(*left*) **Relegated to an express goods working, A4 No.60021 WILD SWAN makes the platform shudder as the driver acknowledges my presence with the chime whistle. Note the old and the new gracing the Grantham platform in the shape of illumination - both the old gas lamp and new electric lamp appear to be permanent fixtures.**

The rain has stopped and the puddles are receding - all we need now is some sun. However, A3 No.60061 PRETTY POLLY appears to be trying its best to obscure the natural light - perhaps a reflection of its appearance. With no shedplate fitted, the King's Cross A3 is perhaps anticipating its imminent reallocation to Grantham where its stay was to be brief as it was withdrawn when the depot closed. A week later it entered 'The Plant' and was never seen again.

By April 1963 the external condition of the A3's in general was nothing short of deplorable. Witness No.60073 ST GATIEN here entering Grantham from the south with an express on 16th April. However, this A3 was allocated to Gateshead where engine cleaners had been in short supply, it seems, since LNER days. No.60073 had not had a boiler change since February 1960 and was due a 'General' at any time now but, it was not to be. Withdrawn in mid-August, the Pacific went to Darlington works for scrapping at the end of that month after spending the whole of its BR career on Tyneside. Note that the sun has at last come out to play, albeit somewhat late.

Whilst I was waiting for my train home I managed one last shot before leaving Grantham. A4 No.60007 SIR NIGEL GRESLEY rushed through the station with a northbound express as admiring glances soak up the fast disappearing scene. The winter had been a long and hard one and it was still chilly even in mid April but that bitterly cold winter probably gave us enthusiasts a breathing space in which to observe ECML steam power for a while longer than was originally planned by the authorities. Diesel failures had been thick and fast and many stored and even withdrawn steam locomotives were reinstated to pull the Controllers out of the mire.

En route to Peterborough (North) from my home in Nottingham necessitated a change of trains at Grantham so whilst waiting for my train on the Up main platform I strolled to the north end knowing I had some time to spare. The day was warm and sunny and the previous winter was a distant memory. The trees were in full bloom and so was the Summer Timetable with all the extra trains run on a Saturday. My first picture of the day was of this New England V2, No.60950, with a southbound express goods. Like No.60948 seen earlier, this engine had also undertaken a short residency at Grantham shed in the summer of 1962 before going to New England. It would also tread the same path to Doncaster and its eventual demise, becoming on of the fifty-five.

Here comes a train with one of my favourite locomotive types in charge. A3 No.60044 MELTON, has a short train this time - only 10 on - so should make light work of the trip southwards. Rebuilt from Class A10 in September 1947, MELTON spent two and a half years working on the former Great Central main line in the mid-50's before moving to King's Cross in March 1956. I remember it well, working the Manchester- Marylebone expresses. It resided at Grantham during the winter period of 1956/7 prior to moving back to London.

My third and final visit to Grantham in 1963 took place on 7th September. It was a day when everything changed forever there because the motive power depot was closing at midnight. PRETTY POLLY looks anything but what the name might suggest and although still in steam here outside the shed entrance, it has worked its last turn and would be condemned the following morning purely by dint of being surplus to requirements. Rain has once again tried to dictate my photographic exploits but I was not to be put off. However, the gloom had set the scene and I suppose No.60061 filled in with the 'doom' bit.

No its not slime decorating the top of the boiler and smokebox of O2 No.63928, its rain. This was yet another engine idling out its last day in service. On Sunday morning it too would be condemned. Note the 4200 gallon Group Standard, flush-sided, tender attached to this engine, number 5619, it was coupled in July 1961, its seventh tender since building, and went with the engine when the whole ensemble was sold for scrap to W.Rigley whose scrapyard at Bulwell Forest was within walking distance from my home, so I was to meet up again with this engine and some of its compatriots. During that fateful weekend Grantham had nine of its O2's condemned whilst eleven others moved to either Retford or Doncaster sheds - a move which was basically a wasted exercise because two weeks later all eleven had been withdrawn.

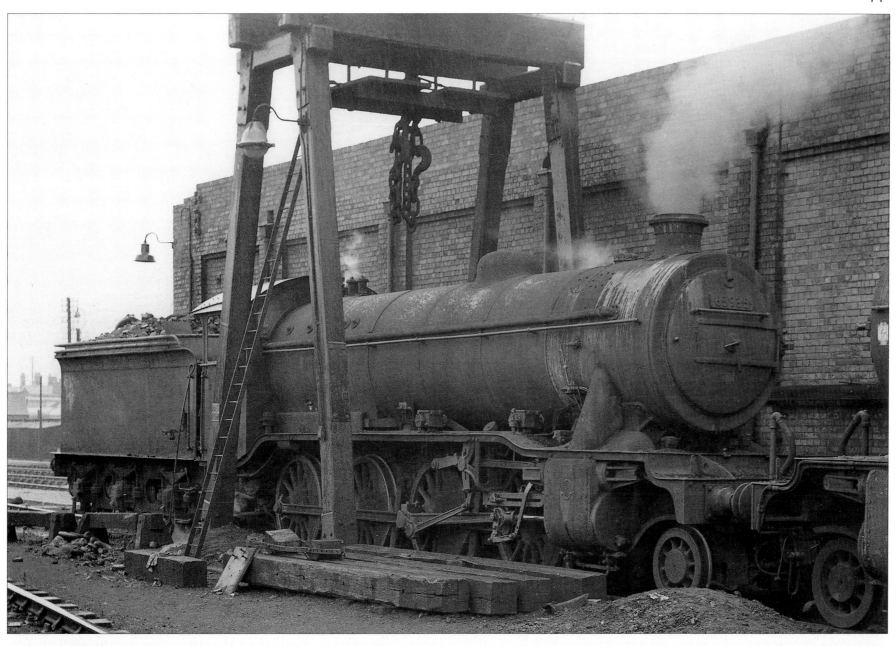

The main employment for the O2 class at Grantham shed was on the High Dyke to Scunthorpe and the High Dyke to Aldwarke iron ore trains and the allocation usually comprised about twenty of these powerful 2-8-0's. Besides the main line duties, some of the O2's were diagrammed to work the single track routes from the main line to the mines. However, that was now recent history on this wet 7th September 1963. No.63935 might be under the sheerlegs but it was still in steam and ready to work. Alas, it was not to be and this O2 was amongst the five Grantham engines sold to my local scrap metal merchant after its Sunday withdrawal. The attached tender was one of the ex-Great Northern 3500 gallon types numbered 5120. It was the sixth and last tender coupled to 63935 and would go with it to Nottingham.

My final photograph at Grantham shed with O2 No.63942 having the honour of posing. Five of the depot's O2's had already been withdrawn and sold during the previous December and once the Doncaster and Retford examples had succumbed in November, the O2 class would cease to exist. This one, withdrawn on Sunday 8th, went to its birthplace at Doncaster for cutting up. The tender, No.5046, was another of the 3500 gallon GNR types which hung on to the end.

For the last view of this ECML sequence I present 'Castle' Class No.7029 CLUN CASTLE in its now familiar preserved condition working a special on the East Coast Main Line on the last day of September 1967. I saw this engine at Swindon in 1965 working a Gloucester bound train and it was in a terrible external condition. What a difference the reversion to Great Western livery has made. Even the coal appears to be hand picked, and the sun is shining. Perhaps the fact that the engine is traversing a proper railway has given it a spiritual lift. Here, shortly after 10.00 a.m. the train sets out for the north after a stop at Newark.

(opposite) **On 11th May 1963, whilst waiting for a special to arrive from St Pancras, traffic at Derby continued unabated and the Bristol-Newcastle express arrived behind Bristol Barrow Road 'Jubilee' No.45690 LEANDER. Passing the North box after its station stop, the 'Jubilee' strides out to its next stop Chesterfield. This engine was only allocated to two engine sheds throughout its life - Crewe North from new in March 1936 to September 1947 when it changed allegiances and moved to the former Midland shed at Bristol. Withdrawn in March 1964, this is now one of the preserved examples of its class.**

The special I was waiting for on that Saturday 11th May 1963 was a joint railtour organised by the Railway Correspondence & Travel Society and the Locomotive Club of Great Britain, from London (St Pancras). On arrival at Derby (Midland) it had at its head 'West Country' No.34006 BUDE, one of the unrebuilt examples which alas was not amongst those later preserved. The Nine Elms Pacific was not 'turned out' too well but by then the south London shed was somewhat short of engine cleaners. No matter, it was nice to see one of my favourite locomotive types away from Southern metals and not too far from my home town. Note the extra long smoke deflectors fitted to the engine for the 1948 Locomotive Exchanges.

The motive power which took over from the 'WC' for the northern section of the tour was Thompson B1 No.61004 ORYX which, although not immaculate, had at least been treated to a cleaned smokebox door. Here the Canklow based B1 is about to get underway from Derby.

Saturday 31st August 1963 was Derby works Open Day. It was also a busy summer Saturday for the station staff with lots of extra trains such as this holiday extra from the south-west which had just arrived behind 'Jubilee' No.45620 NORTH BORNEO, one of the newly acquired Burton 'Jubilees'. Your first impression of this photograph is that none of the young trainspotters are taking any notice of the 'namer'. Did they not realise that exactly five years hence this form of motive power on a BR train would be a memory? Actually everybody was looking across at immaculate 'Duchess' 46251 in the works yard so they could be forgiven. However, my point is that we were lucky in observing and experiencing all that frenzied yet controlled activity of a busy summer Saturday on British Railways in the days of steam - what a glorious time that was when we could ignore the likes of 45620 to look at another similar but new arrival, and take photographs.

Trips to Derby locomotive works were always worthwhile and on Sunday 28th October 1962 I bagged BR Standard No.75009 which was just finishing a 'General' at which time it was also fitted with BR type ATC. A fresh coat of paint has still to be applied but this would stand it in good stead to become amongst the handful of BR steam locomotives operational to the end in August 1968. This engine had been allocated to Templecombe shed on the old Somerset & Dorset prior to its Derby visit and after completion of the overhaul it was transferred to Machynlleth (it is funny how old habits die hard because before the Western Region took over the S&D line, all the old Midland locomotives at Templecombe, indeed those on the S&D, used to travel to Derby for heavy maintenance - perhaps it was just coincidental in 75009's case). Note the chalked 'F' (for front no doubt?) on the chimney and the clean works plate.

Also in the works yard on that October Sunday in 1962 was Fowler 2-6-4T No.42388 which had arrived from Swansea East Dock for a very different reason - scrapping! Built at Derby and starting its operational life at Watford shed in July 1933, the Cl.4 tank moved north to Stockport Edgeley in December 1934. Three months later it went to Longsight for eighteen months and then returned to Edgeley for a twenty year residence. South Wales beckoned in July 1955 and it went Swansea Paxton Street but when that establishment closed in August 1959 it went first to the Great Western shed at Landore but was ejected from there with all the other steam motive power in June 1961 when conversion of that shed into a diesel depot was started. Swansea East Dock was its next home, albeit rather cramped alongside all the other steam locomotives trying to find space in the cramped facility. Derby called in October 1962 and here in the works yard it was inspected prior to being condemned. It was cut up at Derby the following month, not quite thirty years old.

(above) In the Locomotive works during that 1963 Open Day it was difficult to find a quiet corner. There was, literally, bodies everywhere. O4 Part 8 No.63881 had just arrived for cutting up after languishing at Darnall shed in Sheffield since it was withdrawn in December 1962. This was another of the O4s purchased by the LNER for £340 from the Government in 1927 and put into traffic the following year. It spent the whole of the remaining twenty years of the LNER period allocated to sheds in the North Eastern area, indeed it was still there, by now at Dairycoates shed in Hull right up to September 1951 when it was loaned to the Western Region for a fortnight. On its return to more familiar metals, it was allocated to Immingham then in 1953 to Colwick. Darnall then acquired it in March 1954 and it resided until withdrawal except for a week in September 1962 when Langwith Junction borrowed it. Besides 63881, Derby also cut up seven other O4s during the summer of 1963, along with seven Thompson O1 class also.

(right) Just outside Derby works on Thursday 13th August 1964 was one of the ex C&HP 'Austerity' saddletanks, No.68013 which was being made ready for a one-way trip to Great Bridge. Withdrawn a week before, the 0-6-0ST had been purchased by J.Cashmore.

(opposite) **My last foray to Derby in 1964 was during the November when, on Monday the 23rd, I captured this scene in the works yard outside the old Midland roundhouse. Three of the preserved locomotives which usually resided therein were, for some reason, stood outside. Perhaps they had been to an exhibition somewhere? Anyway the engines were: nearest, the exLTSR 4-4-2T carrying the name THUNDERSLEY; the Midland Single No.118, and the 2-4-0 No.158A. On the left of the picture the Engineers crane was undergoing a lift test after overhaul. The polygonal roundhouse used to house the relics was opened in 1847 and was typical of the engine shed style then used by the Midland Railway - a truly magnificent building which was in use for stabling locomotives until about 1888 when it was used for storing engines.**

The Midland Single awaits accommodation in the security of the works precinct. Beyond the boundary fence are stabled a really mixed bunch of rolling stock as ever I captured on film in one place. I have no idea as to the function of most of the vehicles except for the more obvious ones. The one behind Thundersley's bunker appears to be a dynamometer car or mobile test unit, behind that a pair of train heating vans. At the station a 'Peak' has just rolled in from Sheffield with a southbound express.

In the summer of 1959 my late friend Peter Edgington photographed this Burton based 'Crab', No.42799, doing a spot of carriage shunting at Derby (Midland). The 2-6-0 had been at 17B since July 1950 and had got there after a five year stint at Saltley. One of the Crewe built batch, and coming into traffic as 13099, this engine had been allocated to Derby shed when new in December 1927 and managed a thirteen year residency until transferred to Spital Bridge shed in Peterborough during June 1940. Another wartime move, in October 1944, sent the engine to Fleetwood but 'twas only there for a month before going south to Wellingborough. At the cessation of hostilities No.2799 went then to Saltley. Altogether the 'Crab' was allocated to Burton for twelve years before moving on to Nottingham for a period just exceeding two years. From then onwards it was downhill to withdrawal in January 1965 via Bolton in May 1964 followed by Gorton in October, its last shed. It was sold for scrap to Cox & Danks at Wadsley Bridge. *The late Peter Edgington.*

Carefully threading its way out of No.6 platform at Derby (Midland) in the summer of 1959, Saltley Class 5 No.44962 takes a southbound express through London Road Junction. Platelayers are putting the finishing touches to the new trackwork at this end of the station, after the remodelling of the past few years. *The late Peter Edgington.*

By March 1965 most of the passenger services passing through Derby (Midland) had been taken over by diesel power and the 'namers' were in fast decline but parcels and goods traffic could still bring steam locomotives ready for the camera. This is Warrington Dallam based 9F No.92124 which, on 27th March, was waiting for a signal to proceed south with its short parcels train. The 9F had only just transferred to Warrington after a year at Kettering. Prior to that the 2-10-0 had been at Wellingborough since new in March 1957. Even though No.92124 outlived many of the other 9Fs, its withdrawal in December 1966 meant that it never even reached its 10th birthday.

With not much longer in traffic before its withdrawal, Stanier 8F No.48198 drifts through Derby station with a train of 24½ ton mineral wagons en route to one of the numerous Derbyshire collieries still operational on this seventh day of April 1965. The 2-8-0 had been allocated to Derby shed since May 1959 and during that time had seen the depot demoted in status from 17A to 16C. Having spent all of its life, since delivery from the North British Locomotive Co. to Normanton shed in June 1942, working from former Midland Railway sheds, 48198 had only been resident at four other depots during its short twenty-three year life. From Yorkshire it went to Wellingborough in December 1944 and except for a few weeks loan to Kettering in 1956, had nearly thirteen years at 15A. After that it went to Heaton Mersey in March 1957 prior to moving to Derby. It was cut up at T.W.Wards, Beighton.

Barrow Hill based Ivatt Mogul No.43080 had an even shorter future ahead of it in April. Following the 8F through the station with another load of mineral empties, the 2-6-0 was taking part in a parade of the damned and had just two months left before being condemned and then sold to the same scrap merchant but being delivered instead to their yard at Killamarsh. As can be seen this was another of the M&GN based Cl.4's which since closure of that line had fallen on hard times. When new from Darlington in October 1950, this engine went to New England and in February 1954 moved across Spital Bridge shed where it carried on its M&GN tasks. Transferred to Boston in December 1957, it worked on the opposite side of The Wash until December 1962 when Colwick took it in. With much of its work on the former GN route to Derby gone, No.43080 moved north to Staveley in January 1965.

My last visit to Derby, as far as this album is concerned, took place on Sunday 6th March 1966 in order to photograph A4 No.60019 BITTERN hauling this Williams Deacon's Bank Club special into Midland station from Stockport. The working. I beleive, came via Crewe, Stoke, Uttoxeter, North Staffs Jct. (at Willington) into Derby. After turning on Derby shed it returned from whence it came. A4's working in England were by now as rare as the proverbial rocking horse *.*, and Aberdeen based 60019 had been brought down from Ferryhill shed especially for this particular job. The all Stanier LMS rake of carriages behind the A4 look somewhat strange after being used to the Gresley, Thompson and BR Mk.1 types. It was heartening to see the large turn-out of enthusiasts on Derby station that day, no doubt that the planned Sunday working had been a blessing because I'm sure that the Saturday public would not have relished the milling throng of camera-clad fanatics.

As a small child I used to watch the Nottingham to Derby (Friargate) trains pass near to my home in Basford and as soon as I got the chance to use the service myself I was a regular 'punter' commuting to and from Derby Technical College for six months. Having two main routes between Derby and Nottingham, the former GN route was by far the more scenic and interesting, if perhaps less busy. On Thursday 17th October 1963 I decided to take my camera along on my travels to Derby because the cessation of the ex-GN line passenger services had been muted. My first presentation is of Ivatt Mogul No.43065 at Friargate after arrival on a stopping train from Nottingham. Colwick shed supplied the motive power for these services, the former sub shed at Friargate which, up to 1955, had merely been somewhere to stable locomotives overnight prior to them working the first morning services. These 2-6-0s eventually dominated the passenger services on the line and a large number of them ended up at Colwick. No.43065 started life at New England in November 1950 but went in March 1953 for an eighteen month stay at Neasden before returning to Peterborough. Boston had it from December 1957 until it reallocated to Colwick in December 1962. Its withdrawal in January 1965 saw it purchased by scrap dealer T.W.Ward who dismantled and cut up the engine at their Beighton yard.

For the return to Nottingham that particular day, the train engine was No.43154 working tender first because the turntable at Friargate shed was now no longer available having been taken out of commission about 1959 when the engine shed ceased to be used as a signing on point. Note the tender is still fitted with tablet exchanging apparatus from the period when this locomotive worked on the Midland & Great Northern Joint line and was allocated to Melton Constable shed from new in December 1951. When the M&GN closed the mogul went to Boston for a month but before taking up its first residency at Colwick in March 1959 for six months. Its next shed was Lincoln where it stayed for three years before moving back to Colwick, its final shed. Withdrawn in December 1964 it was sold for scrap to an amalgam at Ickles, Rotherham.

The last day of passenger workings from Derby (Friargate) occurred on 5th September 1964. This is the last train ready to depart to Nottingham at 22-10. The motive power was one of Colwick's ubiquitous Ivatt Moguls, No.43160, another former M&GN engine which eventually ended up at Colwick in August 1961. Gas lamps were the only form of illumination although I did set up some flash to help capture the mood. Final trains were 22-10 from Friargate and 22-30 from Nottingham which returned empty stock from Derby. So, those wanting a last round trip travelled on the 20-30 from Nottingham and returned on the 22-10 with a handbell tolling throughout the return trip! The last Derby-Nottingham train was passed near Kimberley by the 22-30 from Nottingham with much exchanging of whistling taking place.

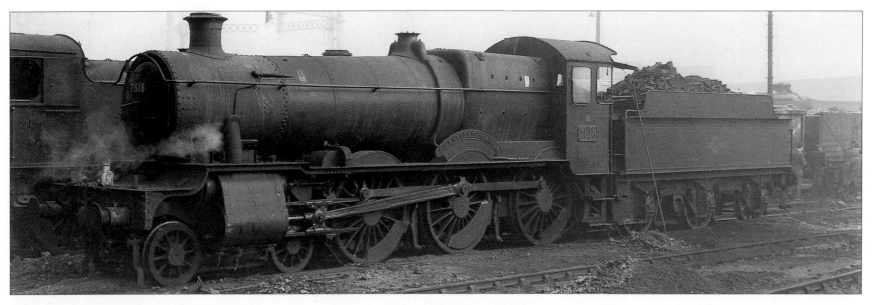

Wolverhampton Stafford Road engine shed 84A - 24th February 1963 (we did the works too that day but took no photographs), 'Manor' No.7818 GRANVILLE MANOR was over the ash pits, or fire pits as the GWR called them, having worked in from Tyseley, its new home since completing a heavy repair at Swindon during the previous November. Assured a few more years because of that overhaul, 7818 worked until January 1965 and was sold for scrap to the local Cashmore's yard after withdrawal. To the right of the picture, plodding through the piles of ashes, can be seen my fellow enthusiasts making their way towards the prize of the day, a clue to which is given by a sheeted chimney visible above them.

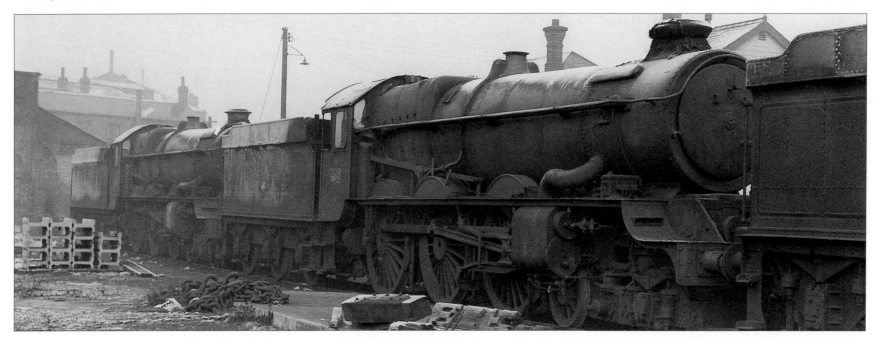

This is No.6014, the original semi-streamlined King which kept the V-shaped cab from those days in the 1930's. The so-called streamlining was neither successful nor elegant and within months of its full application in March 1935, it was being removed bit by bit. However, it was September 1944 before the penultimate section was removed and replaced by conventional splashers. Something must have stuck from that ill-fated experiment though; just look at the 'Counties'.

(*opposite*) Nameplates, numberplates, shedplates, even the smokebox door handles had been removed from the condemned 'King's at Stafford Road shed by 24th February 1963. On view for us that day on the north side of the shed yard were Nos.6007, 6012, 6014, 6017 and 6022. All of them had been withdrawn in 1962 and had spent the winter here awaiting their fate. By Easter it would be decided and they were sold for scrap - no preserved engines amongst this lot. From March onwards Cox & Danks pulled basically one engine a month from the yard here and had it transported to their yard at Langley Green. It seems that we got there just in time before the deed began. The bitter cold of that day can be judged by the amount of frost on the dead locomotives.

On that Sunday 24th February 1963, as part of a 'shed bash' we visited Hereford, Saltley, Stafford Road, Stourbridge Junction, Tyseley and Worcester. At this time there was still plenty of Great Western steam working although the run-down had started in earnest and lines of withdrawn locomotives littered many of the depots. Stourbridge Junction depot comprised a square roundhouse shed opened in 1926, replacing a four road straight shed which had stood to the south of this new establishment. Stourbridge, like most sheds during this period, tended to store their withdrawn and condemned locomotives outside in the yard and such was the case, or so it seemed, with these three Pannier tanks on that cold February day. Nearest the camera is 6424 with 8718 in the middle and 6418 up against the buffers. The former and latter locomotives looked to be fairly intact but No.8718 was anything but. Firstly, the tank side was still letter GWR, some fourteen years after the demise of that organisation but, more dramatic than that, the engine was bereft of its coupled driving wheels and stood instead on a pair of what appear to be either pony or bogie wheels. Whatever they were, the axleboxes had been packed up enough to keep the engine at the same height above the floor as its top and tail cousins. The dome cover also lay at an angle away from the dome and I think its chimney was also missing - what on earth had happened? Whatever had occurred to No.8718 was soon put right because it returned to its home shed at Kidderminster and soldiered on until the summer of 1966 before withdrawal and during that time it transferred to Stourbridge in August 1964. No.6424 had recently joined the Stourbridge stud from Severn Tunnel Junction via Hereford and was stabled for the weekend albeit outside; ironically upon its withdrawal in summer 1964 its place was taken by 8718. On the other hand, No.6418, ex Stafford Road shed in July 1962, had recently been condemned.

(opposite) Worcester shed still had a number of these excellent Prairie tanks in February 1963 and would continue to do so until the end of steam working in the area. No.4113 in particular, which had been allocated to Worcester since November 1953, hung on until near the very end and was not withdrawn until Christmas 1965.

At the time of my February 1963 visit to Worcester, the depot had eight 'Castles' allocated, all of them of the latter built 7XXX series. This one, however, No.7006 LYDFORD CASTLE was one of the Old Oak Common based engines which shared the Worcester-London express services with the 85A batch. Note that 7006 was one of those fitted with a double chimney, a modification introduced in 1956. Worcester engine shed closed in December 1965 but by the beginning of that year all the allocated 'Castles' had gone for scrap and diesel locomotives had taken over their Paddington workings.

Collett 2-8-0 No.3820 was a visitor from Didcot and is sandwiched between two of the depots Pannier tanks amidst mountains of ash and clinker. Worcester was supplied with a couple of grab cranes for clearing these piles. Perhaps the Monday morning gang will clear this lot which is already encroaching onto adjacent roads. It is just possible to discern a rail cutting through the bottom of the picture. The 84XX and 94XX tanks came here from Bromsgrove shed where they had virtually taken over the banking duties on the Lickey incline but a couple of exLMS 0-6-0 'Jinty' tank engines still resided at the by now Western Region controlled shed.

The former Great Western engine shed at Worcester was rather cramped, being sited within a triangle of lines which eventually did not allow any further expansion of the facilities. There was in fact two sheds, a four road through shed built for goods engines and a similar three road structure known as the 'passenger engine depot'. This is the latter shed in February 1963 with resident 'Castle' No.7027 THORNBURY CASTLE simmering outside the south portal and ready for its next working to Paddington. In the left background is the 'goods engine shed' with the stabling yard between the two buildings.

During the mid-1960's, Shrewsbury became something of a staging point for withdrawn steam locomotives making their way, or rather being hauled, to the scrapyards of South Wales and the Midlands. On Sunday 27th March 1966, I caught on film this chimneyless and sorry looking Horwich Mogul shunted into a siding for the weekend near the Abbey church. The engine was awaiting onward transit to Bird's Commercial Motors scrapyard at Long Marston where a number of other former LMS types had been cut up. No.42777 had come from Birkenhead shed and had actually been condemned in the previous August. As to how it lost its chimney is unknown but most probably it was 'borrowed' to keep another of the class in traffic. Birkenhead shed, at that time, was the last operational home of these engines in England. Nearly forty years old by the time of its demise, this 2-6-0 had certainly done its fair share of work and was allocated to numerous depot during its life including: Abergavenny, Camden, Crewe North and South sheds, Nuneaton, Rugby, Springs Branch, Stoke and Swansea; some of those places on more than one occasion. To the right, and just getting into shot, BR Standard Cl.4 No.80078 is another withdrawn and condemned locomotive on its way to a scrapyard. However, the scrapyard in question was in South Wales, at Barry. Need I say more. The 2-6-4T was one of no less than fifteen examples of its class which have been preserved. Perhaps the fact that 80078 had recently been allocated to Shrewsbury shed might have had a bearing on its eventual fate. Pure coincidence you might say but see the following caption.

On the same Sunday afternoon I managed to get this view of 'Manor' No.7822 as the sun was rapidly dropping out of the sky. Minus its FOXCOTE MANOR nameplates, numberplates and shed plate, the 4-6-0 was of course withdrawn and destined to travel to Woodham's scrapyard at Barry. Withdrawn at Shrewsbury depot during the previous November, along with 7802, 7812, 7819, 7820 and 7821, No.7822 was one of those eventually preserved along with the aforementioned 4-6-0's. During the preceding month of October another two Shrewsbury based members of the class, Nos.7827 and 7828, were withdrawn and sold to Woodham's from where they too emerged into preservation. Now, was Shrewsbury a lucky shed for certain locomotives or was it all just pure coincidence? For the record, BR Standard Cl.4 tank engines Nos.80072, 80100, 80135 and 80136 have all been preserved and their last depot was - Shrewsbury. Nos.80078, 80098 and 80105 all spent time allocated to Shrewsbury in 1962-63. Other BR Standards with the Salop/84G/89A/6D connection include: 73050, 73096, 73129, 75014, 75029, 78018.

17th October 1964. Venue - the Holmes scrapyard, The Ickles, Rotherham. This new yard was created in 1964 by a company called Peter Wood, which was an amalgamation of Barlborough Metals, Slag Reduction Co. and Steel, Peach & Tozer. This overall view does not capture in the frame all the locomotives gathered here but it does give a good impression of the space taken up by thirty-odd locomotives which are being taken to pieces with virtual surgical precision. Note that many of the fireboxes - the big copper prize for the scrapman - have already been removed, the rest will take a number of weeks to disappear.

One of the more numerous inhabitants of the yard was this ex LMS 4F, No.44286, being stripped of cladding so that the cutters could get to the prize metal of the firebox. We tend to forget that forty-odd years ago it was quite normal for the asbestos cladding around locomotive boilers was treated more like a bed sheet and which was simply cast to one side whilst more important work was carried out during the scrapping process.

Amongst the early arrivals were two 'Merchant Navy' Pacifics, 35002 UNION CASTLE and 35015 ROTTERDAM LLOYD, the first examples of that class to be withdrawn. Sandwiched between the 4-6-2's was a U class No.31793, another victim of the Southern cull. Cutting up of locomotives had finished here by mid-1965 and former passenger rolling stock became the main diet for the electric arc furnaces fed by this yard. No.35015 was one of the Bulleids I never seemed to photograph on the main line so I had to go to Rotherham to get my photograph of it, albeit in a scrap yard!

The 'U' still wearing its numberplate. Amazingly a lot of the engines which ended up here still had their smokebox numberplates in situ. I wonder what happened to them? Note that some wag has chalked the original number 21C15 on the tender of 35015.